Francis Frith's
PAIGNTON

Photographic Memories

Francis Frith's
PAIGNTON

Peggy Parnell

FRITH
BOOK Co

First published in the United Kingdom in 2001 by
Frith Book Company Ltd

Paperback Edition 2001
ISBN 1-85937-374-7

British Library Cataloguing in Publication Data

Francis Frith's Paignton
Peggy Parnell

Frith Book Company Ltd
Frith's Barn, Teffont,
Salisbury, Wiltshire SP3 5QP
Tel: +44 (0) 1722 716 376
Email: info@francisfrith.co.uk
www.francisfrith.co.uk

Printed and bound in Great Britain

Front cover: Victoria Street from Station Square 1912 64718

Acknowledgements

Charles Patterson – History of Paignton – 1952
C. A. Lane – Illustrated Notes on English Church History – 1904
Dorothy Atkinson – Oldway
David Head
Devon & Exeter Institute Library – Memoirs of Coverdale
D. Hook – Pre-Conquest Charter Bounds of Devon & Cornwall – 1994
Hanniford & Rowe – South Devon – 1907
John Pike – Torbay's Heritage – 1993
John Sutton – 70 Years of Life in Paignton
M. Todd – The South West to AD 1000 – 1939
Peter Tully
P. Parnell – Grand Old Lady of Palace Avenue
Paignton Preservation & Local History Society
R. Penwill – Paignton in Six Reigns
Torquay Museum
Torquay Reference Library

Contents

FRANCIS FRITH, Victorian founder of the world-famous photographic archive, was a devout Quaker and a highly successful Victorian businessman, philosophic by nature and pioneering in outlook.

By 1855 Francis Frith had already established a wholesale grocery business in Liverpool, and sold it for the astonishing sum of £200,000, which is the equivalent today of over £15,000,000. Now a multi-millionaire, he was able to indulge his passion for travel. As a child he had pored over travel books written by early explorers, and his fancy and imagination had been stirred by family holidays to the sublime mountain regions of Wales and Scotland. 'What a land of spirit-stirring and enriching scenes and places!' he had written. He was to return to these scenes of grandeur in later years to 'recapture the thousands of vivid and tender memories', but with a different purpose. Now in his thirties, and captivated by the new science of photography, Frith set out on a series of pioneering journeys to the Nile regions that occupied him from 1856 until 1860.

INTRIGUE AND ADVENTURE

He took with him on his travels a specially-designed wicker carriage that acted as both dark-room and sleeping chamber. These far-flung journeys were packed with intrigue and adventure. In his life story, written when he was sixty-three, Frith tells of being held captive by bandits, and of fighting 'an awful midnight battle to the very point of surrender with a deadly pack of hungry, wild dogs'. Sporting flowing Arab costume, Frith arrived at Akaba by camel seventy years before Lawrence, where he encountered 'desert princes and rival sheikhs, blazing with jewel-hilted swords'.

During these extraordinary adventures he was assiduously exploring the desert regions bordering the Nile and patiently recording the antiquities and peoples with his camera. He was the first photographer to venture beyond the sixth cataract. Africa was still the mysterious 'Dark Continent', and Stanley and Livingstone's historic meeting was a decade into the future. The conditions for picture taking confound belief. He laboured for hours in his wicker dark-room in the sweltering heat of the desert, while the volatile chemicals fizzed dangerously in their trays. Often he was forced to work in remote tombs and caves where conditions were cooler. Back in London he exhibited his photographs and was 'rapturously cheered' by members of the Royal Society. His reputation as a photographer was made overnight. An eminent modern historian has likened their impact on the population of the time to that on our own generation of the first photographs taken on the surface of the moon.

VENTURE OF A LIFE-TIME

Characteristically, Frith quickly spotted the opportunity to create a new business as a specialist publisher of photographs. He lived in an era of immense and sometimes violent change. For the poor in the early part of Victoria's reign work was a drudge and the hours long, and people had precious little free time to enjoy themselves. Most had no transport other than a cart or gig at their disposal, and had not travelled far beyond the boundaries of their own town or village.

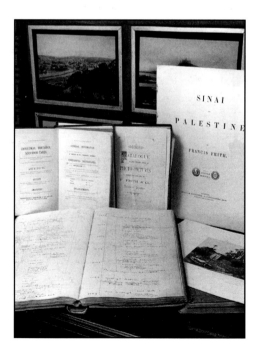

However, by the 1870s, the railways had threaded their way across the country, and Bank Holidays and half-day Saturdays had been made obligatory by Act of Parliament. All of a sudden the ordinary working man and his family were able to enjoy days out and see a little more of the world.

With characteristic business acumen, Francis Frith foresaw that these new tourists would enjoy having souvenirs to commemorate their days out. In 1860 he married Mary Ann Rosling and set out with the intention of photographing every city, town and village in Britain. For the next thirty years he travelled the country by train and by pony and trap, producing fine photographs of seaside resorts and beauty spots that were keenly bought by millions of Victorians. These prints were painstakingly pasted into family albums and pored over during the dark nights of winter, rekindling precious memories of summer excursions.

THE RISE OF FRITH & CO

Frith's studio was soon supplying retail shops all over the country. To meet the demand he gathered about him a small team of photographers, and published the work of independent artist-photographers of the calibre of Roger Fenton and Francis Bedford. In order to gain some understanding of the scale of Frith's business one only has to look at the catalogue issued by Frith & Co in 1886: it runs to some 670 pages, listing not only many thousands of views of the British Isles but

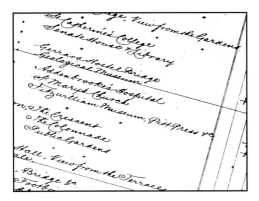

also many photographs of most European countries, and China, Japan, the USA and Canada – note the sample page shown above from the hand-written *Frith & Co* ledgers detailing pictures taken. By 1890 Frith had created the greatest specialist photographic publishing company in the world, with over 2,000 outlets – more than the combined number that Boots and W H Smith have today! The picture on the right shows the *Frith & Co* display board at Ingleton in the Yorkshire Dales. Beautifully constructed with mahogany frame and gilt inserts, it could display up to a dozen local scenes.

POSTCARD BONANZA

The ever-popular holiday postcard we know today took many years to develop. In 1870 the Post Office issued the first plain cards, with a pre-printed stamp on one face. In 1894 they allowed other publishers' cards to be sent through the mail with an attached adhesive halfpenny stamp. Demand grew rapidly, and in 1895 a new size of postcard was permitted called the court card, but there was little room for illustration. In 1899, a year after

Frith's death, a new card measuring 5.5 x 3.5 inches became the standard format, but it was not until 1902 that the divided back came into being, with address and message on one face and a full-size illustration on the other. *Frith & Co* were in the vanguard of postcard development, and Frith's sons Eustace and Cyril continued their father's monumental task, expanding the number of views offered to the public and recording more and more places in Britain, as the coasts and countryside were opened up to mass travel.

Francis Frith died in 1898 at his villa in Cannes, his great project still growing. The archive he created continued in business for another seventy years. By 1970 it contained over a third of a million pictures of 7,000 cities, towns and villages. The massive photographic record Frith has left to us stands as a living monument to a special and very remarkable man.

FRANCIS FRITH's legacy to us today is of immense significance and value, for the magnificent archive of evocative photographs he created provides a unique record of change in 7,000 cities, towns and villages throughout Britain over a century and more. Frith and his fellow studio photographers revisited locations many times down the years to update their views, compiling for us an enthralling and colourful pageant of British life and character.

We tend to think of Frith's sepia views of Britain as nostalgic, for most of us use them to conjure up memories of places in our own lives with which we have family associations. It often makes us forget that to Francis Frith they were records of daily life as it was actually being lived in the cities, towns and villages of his day. The Victorian age was one of great and often bewildering change for ordinary people,

and though the pictures evoke an impression of slower times, life was as busy and hectic as it is today. We are fortunate that Frith was a photographer of the people, dedicated to recording the minutiae of everyday life. For it is this sheer wealth of visual data, the painstaking chronicle of changes in dress, transport, street layouts, buildings, housing, engineering and landscape that captivates us so much today. His remarkable images offer us a powerful link with the past and with the lives of our ancestors.

TODAY'S TECHNOLOGY

Computers have now made it possible for Frith's many thousands of images to be accessed almost instantly. In the Frith archive today, each photograph is carefully 'digitised' then stored on a CD Rom. Frith archivists can locate a single photograph amongst thousands within seconds. Views can be catalogued and sorted under a variety of categories of place and content to the immediate benefit of researchers. Inexpensive reference prints can be created for them at the touch of a mouse button, and a wide range of books and other printed materials assembled and published for a wider, more general readership - in the next twelve months over a hundred Frith local history titles will be published! The day-to-day workings of the archive are very different from how they were in Francis Frith's time: imagine the herculean task of sorting through eleven tons of glass negatives as Frith had to do to locate a particular

See Frith at www. francisfrith.co.uk

sequence of pictures! Yet the archive still prides itself on maintaining the same high standards of excellence laid down by Francis Frith, including the painstaking cataloguing and indexing of every view.

It is curious to reflect on how the internet now allows researchers in America and elsewhere greater instant access to the archive than Frith himself ever enjoyed. Many thousands of individual views can be called up on screen within seconds on one of the Frith internet sites, enabling people living continents away to revisit the streets of their ancestral home town, or view places in Britain where they have enjoyed holidays. Many overseas researchers welcome the chance to view special theme selections, such as transport, sports, costume and ancient monuments.

We are certain that Francis Frith would have heartily approved of these modern developments, for he himself was always working at the very limits of Victorian photographic technology.

THE VALUE OF THE ARCHIVE TODAY

Because of the benefits brought by the computer, Frith's images are increasingly studied by social historians, by researchers into genealogy and ancestory, by architects, town planners, and by teachers and schoolchildren involved in local history projects. In addition, the archive offers every one of us a unique opportunity to examine the places where we and our families have lived and

worked down the years. Immensely successful in Frith's own era, the archive is now, a century and more on, entering a new phase of popularity.

THE PAST IN TUNE WITH THE FUTURE

Historians consider the Francis Frith Collection to be of prime national importance. It is the only archive of its kind remaining in private ownership and has been valued at a million pounds. However, this figure is now rapidly increasing as digital technology enables more and more people around the world to enjoy its benefits.

Francis Frith's archive is now housed in an historic timber barn in the beautiful village of Teffont in Wiltshire. Its founder would not recognize the archive office as it is today. In place of the many thousands of dusty boxes containing glass plate negatives and an all-pervading odour of photographic chemicals, there are now ranks of computer screens. He would be amazed to watch his images travelling round the world at unimaginable speeds through network and internet lines.

The archive's future is both bright and exciting. Francis Frith, with his unshakeable belief in making photographs available to the greatest number of people, would undoubtedly approve of what is being done today with his lifetime's work. His photographs, depicting our shared past, are now bringing pleasure and enlightenment to millions around the world a century and more after his death.

With its wild area of marshy land and rugged sand dunes (see 33638 page 13 and 73070 page 14), Paignton was never really a village, nor did it become an incorporate town like Totnes and Dartmouth. However, it was certainly agriculturally a very wealthy area, as the Saxon Bishops of Exeter knew well when they were given the huge manor and burh in about 1049AD. Around the same time, over 3,000 acres of Devon land was given to the Bishops of Exeter; this was almost certainly intended for the expansion of churches. Christianity had already been well established in the south-west for the best part of 500 years.

In these early days, long before Frith's photographs, the shoreline extended from Polsham, around the old settlement with its pagan mound and ancient cross, along Winner Street, down Fisher Street and out to the harbour (the old quarry). Around the headland of Roundham (Rowneham), further marshlands were partially separated by Goodrington (originally 'Godheres', an ancient site), Sugar Loaf (an Iron Age fort) and Broadsands from the old settlement.

According to the Paignton Urban District Council's records, the manor was still considered an important place during Elizabeth I's reign; at the same time, rudimentary principals of local government were being formulated by the Court Baron and Court Leet. In 1953 it was recorded that 'Paignton during this reign extended to nearly twice the area of the then Urban District', that is, 10,000 acres. Thus the ancient manor and burh of 'Paynton' (the old spelling) has long been a large and very important agricultural town. During Anglo-Saxon times, its rich red soil stretched virtually from the Teign to the Dart and well up towards Haytor, encompassing many farmsteads.

However, the source of Paignton's name lies

Paignton 1889 21524
Site of the original burh.

hidden in the mists of time, and during the past 1300 years its spelling has changed at least 32 times. For many years locals considered that the name originated from 'Paega's-ton' (Paega's farm). Search as one may, this name is not to be found until the 14th to 15th centuries, and the true origin may never be revealed. However, when she was searching through various charters relating to Devon, Della Hook, a well-known expert on charter boundaries, came upon a certain document relating to the movement of cattle between the lowlands and highlands, which included the Anglo-Saxon word for peat - 'paed'. Taking into consideration the common insertion of 'ing' to mean a one-family enclosure and the suffix 'ton' meaning farm, she wondered if it was possible that this could be the origin of the unusual name of Paignton. It is interesting that when Isambard Brunel was laying his rail track in 1858, problems arose due to the subsidence and compression of marsh peat. Again, in the 1990s during excavations for the Inn on the Quay, peat-forming sphagnum moss was found. Taking these factors into consideration, is it possible that over the course of time the sound of 'd' in 'Paed-ing-ton' (meaning peat farm) was softened to 'g', hence 'Pae-g-n-ton', and that the name still later changed to Paignton?

Paignton passed through many changes over the centuries, but the greatest change of all was to be its development as a fine Victorian watering place. But before this could happen much work had to be done.

The Sands and the Pier 1894 33638
If we imagine this scene without the buildings, we can get some idea of the expanse of the marshlands.

Above: View from Primley Hill 1894 33636

Left: Preston 1922 73070
This photograph shows the last of the rugged sand dunes.

It is doubtful if the tough Victorian developers had any idea of the town's past importance, or were even remotely interested in it. Furthermore, it is doubtful whether they understood the influence the Normans had on the Saxon settlement in 1066; the Domesday report showed its potential wealth, including a substantial salt works worth 10d! The Normans, with the assistance of the Saxon Bishop Leofric, set about their enormous task of church expansion, thus drawing scattered villages across the south-west under the wing of ecclesiastical authority. With this aim in mind, almost certainly, they would have erected a mother church on the manor's ancient religious mound.

Evidence of an earlier church was found during repairs to the parish church flooring in 1870: some water-worn stones and rotted oak logs were found, the bark still clinging to the soil. If these were the remains of the cob and thatched Saxon church, and indications suggest they may well have been, then it is likely to have been called St Petrox.

The Normans' colossal church building programme would certainly have started from a pagan or Saxon site; a solid stone building would have been erected in its place as soon as possible. Such a large undertaking would have required a suitable administrative base. Thus what would eventually be the Bishop's Palace was not originally built for pleasure, but as a very necessary business centre; as records show, ecclesiastical work was carried out within the building. There is little doubt that a large number of people passed through the Palace, for huge stables and a tithe barn, larger than Torre Abbey's, are known to have existed.

By the 13th century the manor had become an extremely wealthy centre of crafts and trades. Many examples of the work of the medieval craftsmen can still be seen, not

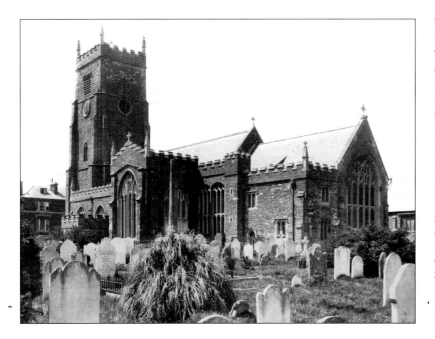

The Parish Church 1889
21533

The parish church is dedicated to St John the Baptist, but it was known in 1488 and in 1755 as the church of SS Peter and Pawle, a name used by the followers of St Augustine in around 600AD. It is moderately larger now than the original Norman building. In the background is the old chapel and nunnery of St Radegun, who was queen of Thuringia in Lower Saxony from 518 to 587AD. In 1823, somewhat altered, the building became the first National School.

only in the parish church of St John, but also amongst the manifold parish churches in the south-west. Often the hand of a single master mason can be recognised. Another indication of the importance of this busy centre is that Paignton had the earliest known bell foundry in England. Furthermore, in 1284 the owners of the foundry, Roger de Ropeforde and his sons and heirs, were granted a house and one penny per annum to make the bells of Exeter Cathedral and to maintain the organ and 'horologe' (an early clock).

So successful were the bishops that on 12 August 1295 their manor and burh was granted one of the earliest market charters, with the right to an annual fair. As was normal practice at this time, the fair took place 'on the fast and morrow of Holy Trinity'.

For many a long year, Paigntonians were known as 'flatpoles' or 'pudding eaters'. The first nickname derives from a certain variety of cabbage for which the town became famous. The second relates to 'white pot', a medieval form of pudding, thought to have been made with cream and known throughout Devon; it was usually given as a token payment to the King for the granting of a town's charter. Perhaps it was the origin of the 'Devonshire dumpling'. Local legend says that the pudding took seven years in the making, seven years in the baking and seven years in the eating, totalling twenty-one years, which rather suggests the period of termination of the charter. In Paignton the period lengthened to fifty years; and instead of being sent to the king, the pudding was distributed amongst the parish poor. In 1859 the custom was revived to celebrate the first train into Paignton, when an enormous pud-

ding weighing twenty-one hundredweight was made. Today the custom is almost forgotten, but it has been revived for some special occasions.

For over 600 years the bishops' manor flourished; next to Crediton, Paignton was considered their wealthiest manor. Because of the bishops' connection, it has always been considered that it cost Paignton dear when Henry VIII dissolved the monasteries in 1547, including the Bishops' Palace. But in reality disease and falling revenues were having a serious effect; also, the bishops' church-building empire was coming to an end anyway. The late Charles Patterson, Paignton historian, points out that it is interesting to note how four years earlier Thomas Fletcher, in his will dated 4 May 1543, had already bequeathed the church of St Peter and St Pawle to 'Peynton'.

Right: The Parish Church, the West Door 1890 25472

The west door of the church, a fine example of Norman work, was removed from the earlier building and incorporated into Bishop Grandisson's extension. On each side of the door are stanchions, which are thought to be for resting a proclamation stage. If that theory is correct, this is where a large glove could have been displayed to open the medieval market and fair.

Left: The Parish Church, the Chantry Chapel 1889 21536

Within the church is a fine chantry chapel, unusual in a parish church. It is thought that Nicholas Kirkham may have built this between 1434 and 1516 not only as a family tomb, but also in gratitude following a spell of insanity. The de Kyrkhames were wealthy, high-ranking people from York and Durham. Nicholas married Agatha Denys of Collaton, and through her the village became known as Collaton Kirkham up to 1630. Here eleven generations of Kirkhams resided, and became involved with important offices in Devon. Their name lives on in medieval Kirkham House (see the drawing above) and Kirkham Street.

The Coverdale Mystery

Coverdale's supposed connection with Paignton has always been something of a mystery. His earlier association with the bible translations and political issues of the day caused him to disappear on many occasions, for Coverdale was a wily man who lived in dangerous times. As a man held in high esteem, he was invited to become suffragan Bishop of Exeter. This was probably because of his extreme wealth and the general impoverishment of the church, but other factors may have also influenced the choice of Coverdale, including the Protestant riots, the rampant inflation and the constant absence of Bishop Veysey.

At the dissolution, the bishops' manor and borough of Paignton was first leased by the bishops in 1545 into the care of Sir Thomas Speke, a member of the Privy Council, who was nominated by the King to hold it for the time being. Four years later, on 15 December 1549, Speke received the manor outright from Bishop Veysey on behalf of the King. With this charter he would have inherited all rights to the manor, as well as the right to wrecks and fishing, including free deep-sea fishing, fishing off Paignton sands, and free fishing off Aish, Stoke Gabriel and Sandridge, along with profits from adjoining parishes and all others within the manor of Paignton's boundary. During his tenure he could well have allowed Coverdale to visit the Palace.

The Vicarage Garden and the Bishops' Tower 1912
64721

The Bishops' Palace building was almost certainly attached to the inside of the curtilage wall; the bishops' tower has long been named by locals 'Coverdale's Tower'.

Then, on 14 August 1551 the Protestant Coverdale was made Bishop - but there were soon more problems for him. Firstly there were two attempts to poison him; later, he was in danger of being imprisoned, but thanks to his wife's relatives he managed to escape, supposedly to Denmark. Then in 1553, whilst preaching the Protestant faith, the news of the Catholic Mary Tudor's accession caused the congregation to walk out on him!

During Thomas Speke's 12 years of involvement with the manor, the Palace could have been more or less intact. Is it possible during these years that Coverdale was glad to use the old Palace or even the tower (64721, page 18) as a refuge? Locals would have been ignorant of the reasons for Coverdale's need of a place of safety, having only heard of this much-mentioned bishop in relation to his Bible translations.

It seems strange that Sir Thomas was given sole ownership of Paignton only to have it taken away eight years later in 1557, when the King granted the estate to Sir William Herbert (Lord Pembroke), who already owned great tracts of land in Wales and Wiltshire. Sir William was a very powerful man who moved in high court circles; he was married to Catherine Parr's sister, and was no doubt held in great favour. Presumably he was granted the manor and borough of Paignton for services rendered to the King.

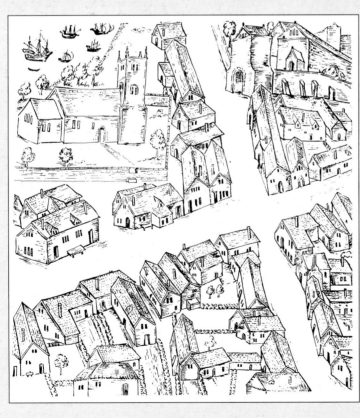

Pembroke's Map of Paignton 1567

On receipt of the estate, which stayed in the family for 87 years, Pembroke took stock of his new manor, and maybe considered the now ageing palace as not worthy of refurbishment.

Later, the manor passed into the hands of another member of the family, Philip Pembroke. Sad to say, Philip became an absentee landlord, along with the many other owners who followed, and between them they allowed the Bishops' Palace to fall into disrepair. It is suspected that the old sandstone blocks found their way into the walls of new buildings along the area beneath the now decaying bishops' vineyards, which was eventually called Winner Street (it was Wynerde Street in 1567).

The Esplanade 1896 38565

In the centre of the picture, by the shelter, is the site of the late 15th-century Torbay House, which was built over an ale house of ancient origin. Houses close to the sea are known to have existed from very early times, and were no doubt places of food and rest for all seafarers.

Nevertheless, the resilient Paigntonians survived. Over time they developed a huge industry in cabbages, which they exported far and wide, even to South Africa; also, with the gradual increase in demand for good old Devonshire cider, apple orchards in vast quantities appeared.

It is interesting that several writers have stated that Coverdale loved his Palace of Paignton. It is also reasoned that as Coverdale was then an elderly man, he could not have travelled the arduous track-ways from Exeter, which went across dangerous Haldon Hill and the Teign marshes. It was indeed most unlikely: in those days, most transportation would have been by water from Exeter to Paignton.

Well before the time of Frith's photographs the Torbay House hostelry (its site is shown in 38565) stood on the shoreline, with an opening onto the beach. It was referred to by Leyland in 1525: 'I mark almost in the middle of the bay one house set on the hard shore and a small peere by it as a socour for fishchar boats'. This has always been considered to be a reference to the old Paignton Pier. Certainly the harbour is known to have played an important part in the trading of fish and tin from the middle ages, but did this strange house have its own pier? A sketch in Ellis's 'History of Torquay' might suggest this. By 1800, Paignton Pier had fallen into disuse. So failing this, Kingswear was the nearest port for Paignton.

The Harbour 1922
73067

From early times, fishing was an important part of Paignton's living and trading. Fishermen regularly brought their creels of pilchards and herring from the creek (Paignton Harbour - see photograph right and P2046, page 24), along the sand bar (Sands Road - see 81150, page 27), to a market space near the Torbay Inn (see drawing below). The name Fisher Street bears evidence to this pathway.

The Torbay Inn

The earliest reference to a harbour was in 1567, when cottages stood on the site of the Gentlemen's Club. These and others like them were known as 'fish cellars', where fishermen and their families lived on the first floor, with cellars for storage open to the sea below; they had ancient rights to lay out their nets on the dunes. The creek had long been called Paignton Pier; it was named from the remains of a structure that once existed there. This creek was possibly made by or enlarged by quarrymen, for the remnants of an ancient quarry are still visible behind the 19th-century houses in front of the custom-house (33646, page 29), which was built to control smuggling and other problems of the time. Nearby, the railings indicate the edge of these quarry workings. By 1621 the harbour was in the care of a 'gardianus de les keys'.

By 1837, the Paignton Quay and Harbour Act received royal assent; soon after this construction started on two quays, costing £3,423 10s. So swift were the builders that in 1839 schooners laden with culm and coal were able to offload their cargoes and reload with cabbages, cider, fish and potatoes. The Harbour Light Café (P2046, centre left) was originally warehouses, and stands where the Key Warden might have lived. During World War I, Mr Gale was harbour master, and in control of necessary war work in the harbour. In 1935 the harbour passed into the hands of the Paignton Urban District Council, and his daughter, Stella Gale, was appointed the only woman harbour master in the British Isles. By the 1960s it was still an active harbour with businesses like Read's Fruit and Potato Merchants (P2027, page 26, right), boat builders, Browse's crab factory (P2027, left) and a sailing club.

The Harbour c1965 P2046

Right:
The Harbour
c1960 P2027

This used to be the path where fishermen carried pilchards and herrings to trade for local produce.

This schooner was registered out of Plymouth. Note the ballast stone waiting to be loaded, and the warehouses in the back-ground. An early catamaran lies alongside the ship.

Another place name with significance is Tanners Lane, Goodrington, with its story of fathomless May's Pool. This pond may well be the site of the treatment of skins in very early times. The story of its depth was perhaps put about to keep locals away from the shallow pool - as it was possibly used to wash skins brought across from the various slaughterhouses. Certainly, cattle were being herded down off the hills into the slaughter yard behind the Crown and Sceptre Inn in Church Street well into the 20th century. One wonders what William of Orange might have thought in 1668 on his unexpected overnight stay at the inn, renamed the 'Crown and Anchor'.

Church Street (64719, page 30) originally Fore Street (the Anglo-Saxon name), was known in the 18th century as Culverhay Street. This name, though not fully understood, almost certainly refers to pigeons. Certainly, behind the present day Coach House Inn (London Inn) there is a 16th-century pigeon-house. However, it has also been suggested that the word Culverhay possibly relates to a Christian cross once situated at the top of Church Street, or even to the huge culverts the bishops used to redirect the Westerland stream in the 13th century, which are still buried beneath the street. But the most likely definition is a dove enclosure or pigeon loft. Near the pigeon-house was once a skittle alley and possibly a bear pit.

Proof of Paignton's very ancient past has been discovered on numerous sites. Important finds have been made, particularly in the 1950s, when Effords Farm House, at the top of Well Street, was demolished to open up Cecil Road. Artefacts uncovered there dated from the late stone age through into the medieval period, and it is possible that the earliest known iron foundry could have been situated somewhere near here.

To the left of photograph 64719 showing Church Street (page 30), and out of sight, are a sweet shop, the old Starkey Knight & Ford brewery (see drawing), the Victoria pub, Well Street, Princess Street (see drawing), the mill pool and the old clink - the latter two are both close to the site of the bishops' mill. Church Street is where the medieval fair was held. In front of the church were the stocks (see drawing), and past the church to the right was the Bishops' Palace. Through the Crown and Anchor archway is the old pigeon loft.

The names Great Gate and Littlegate have long since been thought to refer to lock gates. But it is much more likely that the name came from the Old Norse 'gata', meaning a pathway. These 'gata' or track-ways would have run along either side of the large rivulet that poured out from the Holy Spring; which brought water to the inhabitants and where boats would have been built from very early times. The bishops, in turn, harnessed the crystal-clear water for their Palace and to work their mill. But eventually it was not enough, and they had to bring water down from Westerlands stream. Locals say that in 850 the Danes infiltrated the area of nearby Weekaborough (Wicanbeorg); and were beaten off with great slaughter by the ealdorman Ceorl and his muster of men. (It is also interesting that in the 1970s a late Viking gold twist armlet was found in a rock pool on Goodrington beach. It dates from c1050, and was almost certainly made on the island of Gotland in Scandinavia). (M. Todd, The South West to A.D. 1000, p275-277 1939.)

Above: **The Harbour and the Old Customs House 1894** 33646

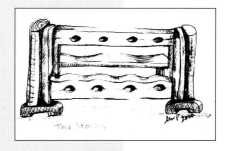

Above: **Starkey Knight and Ford**
Above right: **Princess Street**
Below right: **The Stocks**

Church Street 1912
64719

Old Fore Street, later known as Culverhay, by 1912 was a mixture of architectural styles and had a good selection of shops. The projecting property with the Georgian sash windows was Mrs Martin's Drapery, long since lost to road widening. Opposite is the London Inn, built in 1766. Next door to Macdonald the baker (right) are Evans Engineers, who successfully drained the marshes in 1867. The butchers, with its joints of meat displayed open to the street, was built on the site of the old Crown and Anchor Inn. The courthouse and the magistrates' room were above, and so too almost certainly was Paignton's first theatre!

During the early 17th century prosperity had improved, but towards the latter part the manor passed through the hands of several new owners and became neglected; also, as in so many other towns in England at this time, disease was prevalent. The manor eventually passed into the hands of the Templer family, where it remained until the copyhold system ended in 1922. By the end of the 18th century things had improved considerably. 'Paynton' in 1792 was quoted as being one of the most fruitful areas in the country; unquestionably, there was an abundance of fruit farms and apple orchards. It was possibly due to this that the population expanded. Most houses were small, however, and still constructed of cob and thatch (73069 shows a typical example).

This was the time of the Napoleonic Wars; which caused wealthy Britons to leave their watering places in France and visit the coastal areas of southern England instead.

Above: **Broadsands, Brunel's Viaduct c1965** P2031A

Opposite top: **Cliff Cottage 1922** 73069

Opposite below: **Paignton and Torquay, A General View 1889** 21524

Right: **The Children's Pool and Boating Lake, Young's Park, Goodrington c1960** P2009

Facing the Spanish-style shelter and restaurant, built in 1935, are the remains of Mr Ball's Hospital, and the naval cemetery with its lonely surviving grave. The hospital was closed in 1816. Locals knew the pool as May's fathomless pool. Eventually it was filled in, and a new pool became a popular attraction, particularly in the 1960s and 70s during Children's Week.

The conflict first affected Paignton in 1800: at the instigation of the Admiralty, a hospital (P2009, page 32) was built at Goodrington (the Inn on the Quay). This may well have attracted money and possibly new residents into the area. Some changes in local architecture also appear to date from around this time.

As early as 1832, Paignton was already considered suitable for a summer residence; it had started to show signs of change with several gentlemen's villas beginning to appear. The arrival of 'God's Wonderful Railway' (the GWR) in 1859 (P2031A, page 32) put Paignton firmly on the tourist map, but unfortunately this meant the old settlement would slide into obscurity.

However, it was the Victorian introduction of local government with the Public Health Act of 1848 that was to have the greatest impact. From 1555 Surveyors of Highways existed; as Paignton was of some importance it must have had one, for as late as 1835 a Surveyor of Highways (unpaid) is

Above: New Street and Totnes Road from Winner Hill 1890 25901

This was once the site of the bishops' vineyard. Proof of this was a very old vine found in the grounds of a house in the 1960s, but unfortunately it was removed by new tenants. Immediately below to the right is Palks butchery and the first telephone exchange. Nearby is the Oldenburg Hotel (see drawing), favourite haunt of Prince Oldenburg and his family in the 1850s. Beyond, in the centre of the picture, is the Totnes Road development of 1890, showing the movement away from detached villas to semi-detached houses.

Right: The Oldenburg Hotel

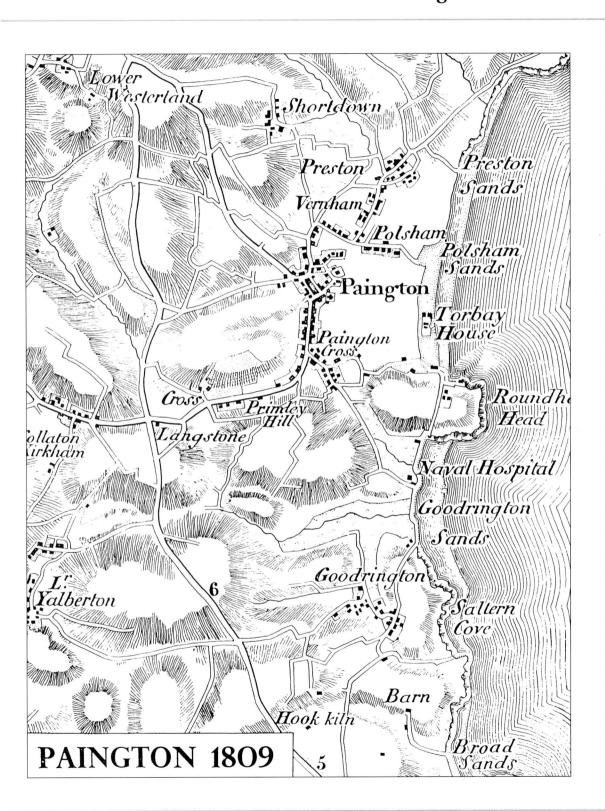

PAINGTON 1809

recorded. Why the parish of Paignton, with its population of some 3,000, did not immediately form itself into a Local Board following the 1848 act is unknown. However, possibly to avoid the 1862 Highways Act, it would appear that by September 1863 Paignton had formed a Local Board of Health with revolutionary plans to clean up the appalling state the town had drifted into. The first meeting of the Board took place in a room over the Crown and Anchor Inn in Church Street, on the site of Pook Bros the butchers (see picture 64719, page 30). This is where the Petty Sessions Division and magistrates' court regularly met, and where the National Schools were endowed.

Meanwhile, the workload increased so much that when the new Local Board of Health started work they had to accept the offer of a room in Winner Street at £5 per year rent, which included cleaning and lighting of fires. During the next five years discussions raged over the erection of a Town Hall to be built at the junction of New Street and Totnes Road turnpike, which led to a lawsuit in Exeter. Meanwhile the Board kept moving between the two rooms until modified plans were finally agreed in 1868. By September 1869 the new building was accepted at a cost of £1,240, and the Board moved into their fine grey granite stone building on 4 July 1870.

Then came the need for a mortuary and lock-up. The clink was by now not in use (owing to the unfortunate death of one of its inmates in 1860), although it was used occasionally as a mortuary. In 1884 a mortuary was erected at the rear of the Town Hall, along with a public convenience. Paignton's first telephone exchange opened in Winner Street in 1885 behind Palks the butchers, with seven subscribers (25901, page 34).By 1901 it was proposed to demolish the mortuary and toilet for road widening. At the same time, a new lock-up and a telephone exchange were conveniently built next door to

the Town Hall in number 3 Town Hall Cottages; the exchange number was 23. Nineteen years later, a manual exchange was installed behind the Palace Avenue Post Office. In 1925 the first automatic exchange in Britain was introduced here; thus Paignton had dial telephones even before London!

In fact, before the Board of Health was formed, much work had already been carried out by the local magistrates. For example, in 1860 they instigated the gasworks in Mill Lane and Churchward Road, thus making possible street lamps in several parts of the town. The gas company's charge for supplying these public lamps was 5/10d per 1,000 cubic feet, and meters were installed on each lamp. The surveyor and a member of the board would read them after lighting periods. The wage for a lamplighter in 1864 was 9s a week (45p today). In 1872 the lamps were 'not lit after the moon was eight days old until the second day after it is full', and then the lamps had to be extinguished 'one hour after moon rise, provided they were out by twelve o'clock'! The magistrates also opened Paignton's first refuse tip in Gubby's Meadow. In 1865 they laid the town's first sewer in Millbrook Street; at the same time a new street was opened out from Winner Street, which is called New Street to this day.

The depression of 1875 had caused agricultural problems, and around this time locals were encouraged by the government to grow more fruit and vegetables. Maybe this is when Paignton's famous flatpole cabbages appeared; or if they had been grown before, they certainly increased, for many were grown on previously reclaimed land, for instance where Palace Avenue is today. Certainly the memory of the flatpole cabbages lingered on into the 1930s and 1940s. Local men took great pride in their enormous specimens, which they now grew on their own allotments; often vying with Herbert

Above: **Preston 1922** 73070

Right: **The Redcliffe Tower 1894** 33645

We can see that twenty-six years after its completion, the sea wall is as good as ever. The tower was known locally as Smith's Folly. It was constructed in about 1854, the dream of an eccentric army Colonel, Robert Smith, a very skilled architect, artist and engineer, who had a long association with India. After losing his wife, he came to Paignton and bought the tower, one of many built in the early 1800s to repel possible French attack. After Colonel Smith's alterations and rebuilding, he was able to liken it to an Indian palace.

The
Redcliffe
Hotel 1907
58419

Whitley (an eccentric millionaire who created Paignton Zoo) in the Public Hall exhibitions held from 1886 onwards.

Originally there was no public recreation area as such, Paigntonians had always enjoyed the freedom to roam the dunes behind the beaches (73070 page 14). Because of this, the area was considered common land, much of which was by this time owned by a developer called Maclain. However, the Board came to blows with Mr Maclain over a portion of land he enclosed, for unknown to him plans already existed to protect the rugged green area for the public.

The great storm of 1866 must have made quite a mess of the dunes, as well as casting up all the shipwreck debris along the coast. It would seem that Mr Maclain threw up his hands at the inundation; in March 1866 he put his 200 acres up for auction. Shortly after this, the Board accepted an offer on his behalf to convey all claims and rights on Polsham Green to them. In so doing they secured Paignton's first freehold public park, with the promise that they would take steps to stop incursions by the sea.

If any development was to take place, there was obviously a need for a sea wall. Consequently, a year later, plans for this and a promenade to protect the green were prepared, which was to be partly financed by public subscription. To the satisfaction of both Maclain and Fletcher, the Birmingham-born developer, a sturdy wall was completed in 1868. In February 1870 there was some local unemployment, so a relief committee paid for local labour at 2/- a day (10p) to lay out the plan conceived by the architects Couldrey and Bridgeman along with two others.

The work ceased at the end of June 1870 with the northern half of the green levelled and seeded and the roads completed, and seats for the green were donated by local residents. By 1874 various sports like archery, polo, cricket and football were permitted on the green (33645, page 37).

A number of people were allowing their cattle to continue roaming on the remaining dunes, and builders were still removing sand. Although the shoreline was not yet owned by the Board, to stop erosion they erected notices by authority of the surveyor to impound any straying cattle, with a reward of £5 for reporting anyone seen causing damage or lifting sand. In 1873 ratepayers had been granted permission to take sand from the Polsham area, providing that they paid 3d a load, and that every load of sand removed was replaced with a load of earth. In so doing the Board were defending the public's rights.

Mr Fletcher and Mr Bridgeman's Story

It was in 1865 that a solicitor called Fletcher arrived from Birmingham, with visions of turning Paignton's dunes into an elegant watering place with grand residences and an impressive esplanade. Intending to build imposing villas, he therefore purchased 60 acres of ground at the southern end of the dunes and marshes, which included Torbay House. This grand residence had an enclosed garden growing all manner of exotic fruits, flowers and vegetables; its pair of grand wrought iron gates was set between two cut pillars, and a high archway faced towards Town Bank. On the seaward side there were wings running westwards and a lawn. A piece of the seaward wall still exists, with signs of a gate onto the sands. Within the walls, archery and other sports were often practised on the grass.

Beyond Torbay House lay only rugged land, in Mr Fletcher's eyes ripe for development. He sought the help of an esteemed local architect, George Souden Bridgeman, a descendent of two of the oldest families in Torbay, a staunch chapel man and creator of many buildings in the bay. Together they drew up their plans. In rapid suc-

Above: **The Club House 1896** 38554

Right: **The Esplanade and Roundham Villas 1896** 38555

Early visitors found Paignton 'select, dignified and discreet'; it was the ideal place for the professional gentleman. In 1881 a clubhouse of a non-political nature was formed. In time, land from the Fletcher Trust was acquired, and Mr Bridgeman's classic design erected. Beach shops now fill the front garden, and there is a car park in the café garden. In the background, built in 1885, is Kingswood (originally called The Quarry), which later (c1910) became the home of Paris Singer's wife. In 1939 the land in front of the clubhouse was obtained, and the promenade extended to the harbour.

cession cabbage fields, apple orchards and sand dunes disappeared, to be replaced with fine villa residences and Gothic terraces.

Following the death of Mr W R Fletcher in 1875, the Fletcher Estates took control of most of the southern dunes and much of the marsh - now Queens Park and the Adelphi area. In 1878

they demolished Torbay House. In 1879 the Board approached the trustees in the hope of purchasing the site as a public open space. Two years later a deed of gift at the behest of the Court of Chancery was signed, and the whole of Paignton Green passed into public ownership with stringent covenants on building.

Development was rapid once all the services were laid and the marshes drained. Within a matter of thirty years, the old manor and borough of Paignton was hidden behind a façade of Victorian architecture.

The first roads on the wasteland appeared in 1863, when the Torbay and Dartmouth Railway Company laid a rough road between Victoria Square, the station (little more than a halt at this time), Station Road (Victoria Street) and Town Bank (Torbay Road). The roads were laid out for the GWR's horse-drawn bus to transport goods and people between Torquay and Paignton stations and Torbay House. The Board quickly insisted that the company make up these two important roads properly. The Board also faced up to the demands that the proposed massive development was going to have on their services: with the arrival of such progressive men as Dendy, Bridgeman and Couldrey, the new town was ready to spread its wings. Along Town Bank a grand row of houses already stood stark against the acres of green fields, known to the locals as 'Streaky Bacon Terrace' (25902, right). Who the people were that moved into these magnificent houses, so

Above: **The View from Belle Vue 1890** 25902

To the centre right we can see Paignton station and Brunel's parcel office. To the right is 'Streaky Bacon Terrace'. Between that and the station can be seen Nelly Pope's railway café, a popular meeting place for the young bloods of the day. Immediately opposite is the Broadmead Hotel, later to become the Picture House (the Torbay Cinema).

very different to the native cob and thatch, can only be guessed at.

Mr Dendy's Story

Of all the entrepreneurs to arrive in Paignton, one of the most prominent was a wealthy young barrister from Birmingham, Mr Hyde Dendy. An astute businessman, he invented schemes for exploiting the advantages that could be gained by reclaiming low-lying areas; he saw them successfully carried through, even though he had many a brush with the Local Board. His first project was the

**The Gerston
Hotel 1907**
58429

Mr Dendy's Bathing Machines 1896 38545

With his powerful business aptitude, Mr Dendy quickly installed the most important tourist commodity, bathing machines; those for the ladies were on Paignton beach, and those for the gentlemen on Preston beach. Alas! Dendy soon discovered that he was loosing male custom. In 1871 a man was prosecuted for bathing near the ladies' machines. Because of this, Dendy fell foul of the Board for not clearly displaying notices regarding the strict by-laws on bathing. The following year he campaigned for a seat on the Local Board and was elected; he became chairman in the following year, and very soon had things altered!

Gerston Hotel (58429, page 44), which was judiciously situated next to the trains. In 1872, he submitted plans for joining two houses, thus creating a grand tourist hotel on the Esplanade - now the Inn on the Green. He also owned considerable land behind Steartfield House. He lived for a while in nearby Parkfield House, gracing his entrance with the gates and pillars from Torbay House. He ran a local newspaper, a bus service, and regular steam launches from his pier to Torquay, and was also responsible for the controversial bathing machines (see 38545, opposite).

Music hall was becoming all the rage, and Mr Dendy reasoned that Paignton should have a suitable venue. So within his Gerston Hotel complex he built his famous Bijou Theatre, and employed a well-appointed stock company which played continuously into the 1880s. The unpretentious entrance was around to the right of the building. Bijou it certainly was. The delightful, elegant room was extravagantly furnished with grand chandeliers and beautiful gilt-framed oil paintings, complete with a mini-stage with a painted backdrop depicting Paignton's future green. The Torquay Directory of the time reported: 'The absence of a Dress Circle and Boxes spoils an otherwise good room'. For all that, this minuscule theatre was to have its moment of glory: on 31 December 1879 the first copyright production of Gilbert and Sullivan's 'The Pirates of Penzance' was performed in the presence of the Prime Minister, Benjamin Disraeli. How the 'royal' appendage to the theatre's name came about in 1874 is not really known, but it was most probably following the attendance of Princess Louise; she always headed Sullivan's party lists, and was a regular visitor to Torquay. Within a very short while Dendy initiated a horse-driven omnibus service between Torquay and Paignton from outside the theatre, with a last bus after the final curtain. The fare was 6d and l/- return.

In Dendy's mind, no self-respecting watering place could be without its pier. To this end he purchased Teignmouth Promenade Pier. However, finding it too impracticable to remove, he had it reinstalled, and then sought the help of George S Bridgeman to produce a suitable design for Paignton. The pier was duly built opposite his Esplanade Hotel, next to the Holy Well outflow. It was opened to the public on 30 June 1879 (see 21529, page 49). It was not what we now think of as a traditional pier with slot machines and 'What the Butler Saw'; these developments came much later. Dendy's pier was a walkway across the water to a fine pavilion, well set up for concerts, plays and sacred music on Sundays, and for special productions - like Gilbert and Sullivan's 'HMS Pinafore' on the water, which was performed here. An adjacent saloon contained two Thurston billiard tables. The pier was a covered way for bathers, and a place for roller skating and leisurely afternoon teas.Sadly, all was lost in 1919 when the pavilion burnt down - and a valuable grand piano from the Bijou Theatre went crashing into the sea.

In his time, Dendy had several brushes with the Local Board. One in paticular was in July 1891 when a proposal was made to acquire the marshes between Hyde Road willow plot and Victoria Road. Mr Dendy's objections caused a compulsory purchase order to be slapped on him. The newly-acquired marsh became known as The Park (Victoria Park). Its progress proved turbulent. This and other factors culminated in Dendy's resignation from the Board. In 1895 a gift of a swan was made to the park, and by 1900 most of the work had been accomplished (44568, page 48). For all that it was Dendy who always said 'Torquay was built for Paigntonians to look at'. Arthur Hyde Dendy died in Paignton on 13 August 1886, but his name and his achievements live on in Dendy Road and Hyde Road.

Hancock's fair was granted use of the park, until complaints were registered about the mess and damage they made. They were moved onto Berry Square and later Paignton Green, and eventually amalgamated with the Regatta fair. Victoria Park was not completed until 1937 and all that remains of the ancient willows is a small area by the library.

The ancient gushing spring that caused so much flooding over generations was redirected underground by the Victorian engineers; it went through the park to create two lakes and a picturesque stream (44568), continuing on underground to finally rise like an icy cold whirlpool by the pier.

Above: **The Pier 1889** 21529

Opposite top: **The Esplanade from the Pier 1889** 21530

Opposite below: **Victoria Park 1899** 44568

Below: **The Pier from the Esplanade Hotel 1896** 38552

This view of the pier, taken seven years after the previous two photographs, shows that Paignton then had interesting shops; advertisements offered Turkish baths, drinking chocolate, a drug store, cleaners, and good old Devonshire cider!

Above: Terra Nova 1889 21532

This building is now the Park Hotel. In front is one of the many bicycles and tricycles that flooded the town.

Opposite top: The Esplanade Hotel 1894 33644

Because of the flat roads, bicycles were in abundance both on the streets and greens, so much so that they caused problems for pedestrians. Because of their popularity and the public's enthusiasm, Dendy built a racetrack at the back of his Esplanade Hotel; we can see the entrance to Dendy's cycle track on the right.

Opposite below: Paignton from the Pier 1925 78470

Langford's tents have now taken the place of Dendy's bathing machines. Opposite is Redcliffe Lodge, and between the trees is Dendy's Parkfield House.

Although one could hardly call Isaac Merritt Singer a true entrepreneur, he certainly was a very wealthy man. Contrary to general belief, he did not actually invent the sewing machine, but amassed his fortune through his ingenious invention of the shuttle and by his amazing salesmanship in America. Eventually he produced his own sewing machines, complete with his patented shuttle.

The Singer story is well-documented elsewhere. However, owing in part to the Franco-Prussian War and in part to the air pollution in London (which affected his wife Isabella's health), Isaac Singer was recommended to move south. Having visited Exeter once before, Singer decided to return to Devon; in 1871 he stayed at a hotel in Torquay to look for a suitable property. Following Brunel's death, his fine estate was up for sale. Singer made enquiries, but the trustees kept making excuses. Apparently they were not keen to have a man with his doubtful reputation living on their manor! Singer was never accepted by Torquay society.

Isaac Singer decided to look elsewhere. Seeing that a desirable estate, Fernham, was up for sale in close-by Preston, he viewed and purchased it. Settling into one of the two houses, Oldway, with his wife and family, he proceeded to remove six cottages and a pub. His main object was to build an opulent mansion. Having seen and admired the work of George Souden Bridgeman, Singer asked him to design a 'wigwam', an American name for an Indian home; it was to include a riding and exercise pavilion. Isaac was a perfectionist: he oversaw each stage, causing the builder many a nightmare, for if something was not to his satisfaction he insisted that it be rebuilt! Singer had quite an effect

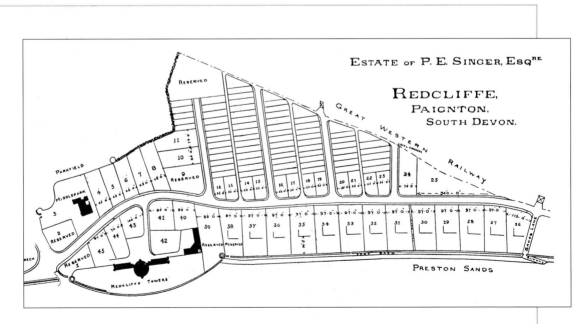

The Redcliffe Estate

Above: The Redcliffe Hotel and Garden 1907 58420

The Redcliffe had a hydropathic plunge bath on the seaward side of the building, connected to the house by a subway that filled with seawater at high tide. Unfortunately, it was washed away in the storm of 1873. In 1900 the Singer family fitted out the Redcliffe Tower as a convalescent home with twenty or more beds for the wounded of the Boer War.

Left: Preston Green 1922 73074

on Paignton, particularly with local trades-
men, who found his wages hard to match.
Singer was a temperamental redhead, but
an extremely generous man. He included
Paigntonians in many of the activities on
his estate, and always made sure that local
children had plenty of goodies at Christmas
time; he even put on a circus in the Rotunda
especially for them. Although at this time
he was over 60 years of age, he still had an
eye for the ladies - and possibly one
Paignton lady in particular!

Sadly, he died just before his mansion was
completed. Ironically, his mausoleum had
to be in Torquay because of its size. His wife
and family decided to live on in the

Top: **The North Sands from the Pier 1896** 38549

We can see the Esplanade Hotel (centre) and Steartfield House (right), the homes of
Mortimer and Washington Singer.

Above: **Oldway c1955** P2010

mansion, keeping an interest in the town. In 1876, as a trustee Isabella Singer was thanked for erecting the Preston sea wall, and for the reinstatement of a footpath across the meadow.

Through a series of events the family returned to Paris. Through another series of events, they all returned to Oldway, and the boys duly settled in Paignton. In 1891 Paris, Isaac Singer's third son, together with his brothers Adam, Mortimer and Washington, founded Paignton's cottage hospital. They gave a field known as the Crofts, on condition that no person suffering from an infectious or incurable disease were admitted! Costing £2,885 5s 9d, it was supported by voluntary contributions until the National Health Service took it over in 1948. The main frame of the building still remains.

In 1893 Colonel Smith's son sold the Redcliffe Estate to the Singer Trustees, who bought it and the surrounding land for Paris - he was 13 years old at the time - with the idea of building grand villas. Paris sold the first plot to Robert Waycott, who built Villa Marina, now a hotel. In 1900 the family had the Redcliffe Tower fitted out as a convalescent home for the wounded of the South African (Boer) war. By 1914 World War I brought Paris Singer's development plans to a stop, but not before he had completed the Marine Drive and the buildings along the west side. The ground got badly churned up with army training and practice dug-outs. Paris eventually offered the land to the Council for £600.

Paris also offered to install electric light across the sea front and in Winner Street, and he was willing to sell the undertaking back to the town at the original price. However, it would appear that the Board were having contract difficulties; they were forced to continue with gas lighting until 1909, when five electric lights were installed across the town.

After their mother's death in 1904, the children decided to sell the Wigwam. Paris bought out his brothers' and sisters' shares, and with his love of French architecture started to put his plans into action to create a house in the style of Versailles (P2010). He took over the Oldway estate from his father's trustees, and in so doing he was instrumental in developing parts of Preston, Oldway and Barcombe.

Paris stopped his rather wayward brother Washington, who was aged 21, from ranching in the far west; for Washington had interests worth over one million pounds. Because of his brother's keen interest in horses, Paris set up a stud for him. One of the horses, Challacombe, won the 1905 St Leger. Washington married and moved into Steartfield House (38549), which he enlarged and improved. Eventually it became the Palace Hotel. The stables and coach house behind have been tastefully reconstructed into retirement flats, which recently won the developer a gold medal award. Brother Mortimer, who bought Washington his first horse, also purchased Dendy's Esplanade Hotel next door (38549).

During Paris Singer's captivation with the world-famous dancer Isadora Duncan, and whilst she was in residence at Oldway, it is said that he moved his wife into Kingswood House (see photograph 38554, page 40); however, as the marriage was already in trouble, she had probably already left. Paris and Isadora were often seen visiting the Picture House in Torbay Road (photographs 38569, page 61 and 25902, page 42). Later, in 1967, Oldway was used for filming 'Isadora' (photograph P2010), which starred Vanessa Redgrave and included many locals as stand-ins.

The Singers were benefactors to the end: it was Washington Merritt Singer who provided blocks of flats for the working families in St Michael's, which are still known as Merritt flats.

After Isadora's death, Paris returned to live in France. Eventually, from 1929 to 1940, Oldway became the Torbay Country Club . Then, as in 1918, it played a part in the Second World War. Finally in 1946 it passed into the hands of the Paignton UDC at the concessionary figure of £45,000.

Preston Sands 1918
68533

Keenly interested in cars and aviation, Paris Singer had his own hanger built on Preston Green. Later Captain Truelove used the hanger to house his Avro seaplane for tourist flights around Torbay.

Paignton, A General View 1894 33637
From Winner Hill, showing the reclaimed marshes.

By 1896, Paignton had become a fully-fledged watering place with leisurely drives along the prom, refreshments on the sands and Hancock's Fair (38558, page 60) - but there are no deck chairs to be seen in this photograph! Development continued unabated, but fortunately the removal of sand came to an end in 1898.

In the same year Paris Singer gave the flagstaff and a Red Indian vane from the Wigwam for erection nearby the shelter. The following year, on the west side of the shelter, a fountain was erected by public subscription to celebrate Queen Victoria's Jubilee in 1897 (33639A, page 60). Both disappeared mysteriously when the Festival Hall was built in 1966.

The 1880s and 90s had been the most prolific period of the marshland development (33637). Electricity was talked about for the town. Christ Church, St Andrews, and Collaton churches and all but the old Methodist chapel were built in this period. The old mill and pond in Well Street were purchased and turned into the town yard. On the green there were a variety of entertainments, like Hancock's and the Regatta fairs, minstrels and military bands, and small shelters to sit in arrived. The new Improvements Association was a great asset in promoting the town as a seaside resort. With a loan sanction, the gardens on the Torbay House site were laid out, and the promenade and shelter were completed. This shelter was supposed to have a bandstand on the roof, but objections were made to the height, so Paignton's first bandstand was built on the sea wall (see 38565, page 21). However, it was so small that successive bands preferred to play on the shelter roof instead! The problem of height was to arise again eighty years later.

In 1886 Palace Avenue was still growing Paignton's famous flatpole cabbages, whilst in Victoria Street cows innocently grazed nearby the wooden railway bridge. Work on the Esplanade drew to a close. It could be said that

Victoria Square was the heart of Paignton's new town. Some time between 1809 and 1863, an early cluster of buildings appeared in a field called the Gerstons. One of the first was the Gerston Inn, built in 1846, sited at the junction of the Torquay, Dartmouth and Totnes turnpike; by 1849 it had become the Commercial Inn (and was later Greens Hotel, the Moors and the Coverdale). In 1859 a terrace of four houses was built next to the Bishops' Tower (38572, page 62) for the railway engineers. Further along is Gerston Terrace and Gerston House.

Later, when Mr Foale opened his butchery business on the corner of Victoria Square and Station Road (Victoria Street), he set a precedent by giving 10ft of his land to the Local Board for a footpath; thereafter all successive shops, more or less, did the same. Within a very short time a variety of private and multiple shops appeared. By 1899 a public transport system between Torquay and Paignton had been introduced.

Waycott is an old Paignton family name; the Waycotts were brewers, house agents and furnishers. One Robert Waycott was in the 1930 Operatic Society's production of 'The Yeoman of the Guard' at the Public Hall/Theatre. Unfortunately their fine corner building we can see on the right of 64718 (pages 62-3), named Waycott's Corner, was destroyed by fire in 1952.

Right: The Esplanade 1896
38558

Below: The Jubilee Fountain 1894 33639A

Opposite below: Torbay Road 1896 38569

The large shelter and the Jubilee fountain replaced the grand wrought iron gates of Torbay House as the focal point of Torbay Road. By 1896 it had become an elegant residential road with just two or three plots left; here Mr Lamshead's famous Deller's café would be erected in 1910. At the top of the road was the Broadmead Hotel, the future site of Paignton's Picture House (the Torbay Cinema) which followed. Today, this delightful cinema is a grade II listed building. It was still running in its original state until it closed down in 1999 - a unique piece of living history was lost! In the background was the Marist Fathers' House, prominent on the hill with its white statue of St Mary.

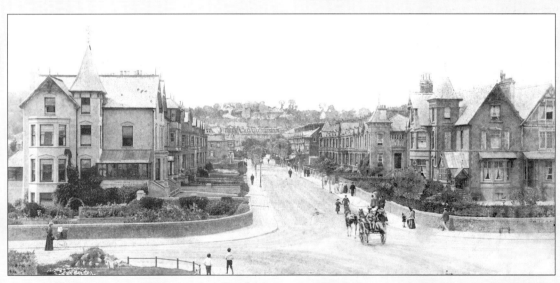

Opposite top: **The Palace Tower 1896** 38572

Above: Victoria Street from Station Square 1912 64718

A motorised bus waits for shoppers in Station Square alongside the horse-drawn cabs. Cabbies' fares at this time were: 'Drawn by 1 horse or 2 ponies or mules - One hour or less 3/- (15p) or extra half hour or less 1/6d, 1/- a mile. To Southfield 6d extra. To Primley Park 6d extra'. Horses were well catered for with a water trough and built-in toilet facilities!

Opposite below: **Two advertisements from the 1900s for Palace Avenue businesses**

The Palace Estate

From the start, the future design of Paignton's new town had been in the hands of two ingenious men, George Souden Bridgeman and Walter G Couldrey, who were both destined to have a profound effect on Paignton's development over the course of thirty years. Their brilliantly conceived plan for the business centre of Paignton (see the Estate Plan opposite) was their ultimate achievement.

The closure of Dendy's Bijou Theatre had caused some disquiet amongst the public; a place of general entertainment was needed. Arguments raged over the position of the proposed public hall. Finally, an agreement was reached to place it at the top of Palace Avenue (38575), but unfortunately with the entrance facing away from the road. The reason for this was possibly the fact that Palace Avenue was built on sand and was subject to constant flooding.

Once the estate was finally laid out, well-established businesses in Winner Street began to move into the Avenue. One enterprising entrepreneur was a Mr Lambshead, whose Deller's Supply Store, established in 1844, was

The Gardens and the Wesleyan Chapel 1896 38573

Looking from the Hall (or the Palace Avenue Theatre) through the gardens, we can see Norton's and Welton's shoe shops. On the right is the new police station, with the Petty Sessions Division and Magistrates' Court (later demolished). Further down is the Post Office, erected in 1889. At the toe of the garden is the town's tribute to the men and women who lost their lives in two world wars (73066, page 68), some of whom may well have started their training as volunteers in the Drill Hall under the Public Hall/Theatre.

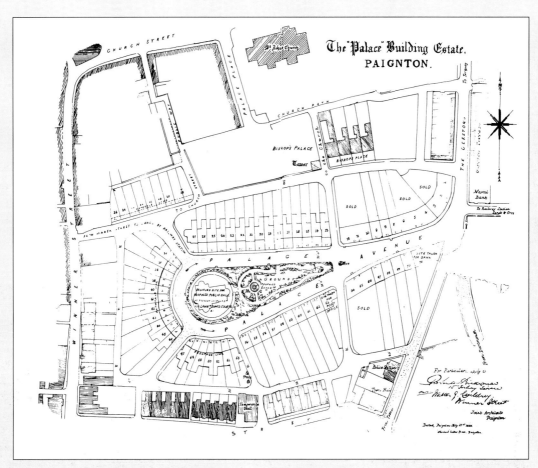

Above: The Palace Estate Plan 1886

Left: The Public Hall 1896 38575

This Victorian edifice has been the venue for all manner of entertainment for all kinds of people over the decades, particularly as a repertory theatre. Operatic and dramatic groups, pantomime and various festivals which put on many good shows. Then during World War II the Public Hall was a garrison theatre for our servicemen and women and for the thousands of American troops stationed here prior to the D-Day landings; they had many famous artists to entertain them, including Anna Neagle, Glen Miller and almost certainly Bing Crosby.

the first to install electric lighting (see 58418, page 68, right). Amongst many other of his interests, he not only opened a large store in Palace Avenue but also another in Torbay Road. He was closely followed by Rossiters Costumiers & Drapers, who opened a double-fronted shop in No 7, and installed their own street lighting. Ellis's the ironmongers and the Torbay Printing Works, better known as Axworthy's, also decided that the Avenue was the place to be. But still the Local Board insisted on keeping their 'fish tail' gas lamps!

The life of the Local Board was 31 years 3 months, and in this time they saw the population increase from 3,000 to 7,000. They met for the last time on 29 December 1894. As a parting gesture, they succeeded in purchasing a section of Paignton's marsh to develop what became Victoria Park. Two days later, the Paignton UDC took over the town's administration until the creation of the County Borough of Torbay in 1968.

Through arbitration and a public vote the PUDC, with the help of the Paignton Improvements Association, managed to secure Mr Mallock's marshes for the development of Queens Park, named in honour of Queen Victoria's Jubilee, at the cost of £6,000. Work was begun in 1900, with the help of a loan sanction of £2,500. After 3,000 loads of earth, which had been obtained for 10d a load, had been delivered, the erection of a grandstand and pavilion began. By May 1901 the Gardeners' Association was allowed to use the green.

Over the course of the next few years the park was completed. By 1907 it was in full use, as the programme on the lamp-post in Victoria Square suggests (see 58418, page 68) - a packed timetable of sports offers tennis, croquet, bowls, archery and cricket.

Palace Avenue 1896 38571

This view looks towards Victoria Square. Opposite Foale's butchery was the Naval Bank, which eventually became Maypole

Corner with its glitzy gilt and glass sign-board. On the right, opposite Deller's Store, is the scientist Oliver Heavyside's family business - we can see the sign advertising pianos for hire. Oliver spent much time in his room above his brother's music shop working on electromagnetic theories that culminated in his discovery of the Heavyside Layer, named after him.

Right: **Palace Avenue 1907** 58418

Below: **The War Memorial 1922** 73066

Expanding Victorian development brought some problems to Paignton. For instance, in the early 1900s there were regular complaints about the Salvation Army band, numerous other bands and entertainers on the Green.

The Regatta fair always drew protest from residents, as it does even to the present day. Nevertheless, Donkey Daniel's donkey rides and Punch and Judy continued to delight the children, and ice creams and beach photography were popular - we can see a beach photographer's booth just to the left of centre behind the wall in 38560. Trams, motor cars and motor buses, as well as bicycles, added to the enjoyment of a holiday in late Victorian Paignton.

The first deckchairs appeared in 1901. A regular Beach Inspector was employed in 1910 at the wage of 21s 0d per week. He was assisted by a youth or retired pensioner to help pack Mr Langford's deck chairs in the main shelter at night.

Above: The Pier and the Sands from the Esplanade 1896 38560

Right: The Promenade and Sands 1907 58415A

The Greens
1925 78481

The Sands 1925
78479

1925 saw a part of the south green made into a bowling green, and three years later a rather rough, but functional putting-green was made next to it. Boat trips off Paignton beach gave toddlers much fun walking along the landing stages.

Above: **The Sands 1925**
78480

**Opposite top: The Sea Front
1912** 64711

The site of the eventual
canvas covered tent.

**Far left and detail near left:
The Sands and the Pier
1925** 78476

Negotiations over the beaches were finally brought to a conclusion when the Duchy of Cornwall agreed the sale of the Paignton, Preston and Goodrington foreshores; the latter stretched around into Fairy Cove and under Roundham Head. Here, in 1935, government sponsorship for unemployed miners from south Wales enabled the creation of the popular rock walk. The late 1930s were a busy period for the acquiring of coastal lands and beaches. Unfortunately, the purchase of Broadsands (P2031) had to be shelved until after the war. At the same time the pier was cut in half, hotels and the gas works installed gunnery emplacements, and to deter any would-be invader, thousands of miles of barbed wire were extended along the beaches.

By the end of the war, the rock garden around the Jubilee fountain had matured. Coloured lighting was installed, turning the rockery into fairyland in the dark. The canvas-covered bandstand (built in 1926), where Charles Shadwell's orchestra kept our spirits up during the war with 'Roll out the Barrel' and the like, was in 1953 renamed the Summer Pavilion under the town's first Entertainments Manager, Harold Bultz. This is where some of Britain's most famous artists made their first stage debut whilst raindrops kept falling on their heads!

Gone now are the acres of Paignton's cabbages (see 25903, page 81). Gone are the pierrots on the Green. Gone is the Adelphi Theatre of 1908, with its corrugated walls and roof and memories of Albert Sandler's orchestra, Claud Hulbert and Norman Evans of 'Over the Garden Wall' fame. Gone also is Hancock's fair and bioscope. The terrace houses in Torbay Road are now transformed into food shops, dress shops,

Right: **The Sands, Preston c1955** P2017

In the background is Hollacombe Gas Works. The retaining wall along Torquay Road was the 1886 halfway meeting place of the 'Flatpole' and 'Dicky Bird' bands of warring youths! In the centre is St Paul's Church, built in 1939.

Below: **Broadsands c1965** P2031

gift shops and Olympia fruit machines (P2044). Restaurants too have come and gone, in particular Deller's Cafe, the pride and joy of Paignton (58417A, page 82); it is heart-breaking that it was demolished in 1965, to be replaced by a terrace of grey concrete block gift shops! Still standing on the Esplanade, but long forgotten, is Deller's Summer Café (81153A, page 82). Bed and Breakfasts, guesthouses, small hotels, campsites and residential houses mushroomed - and so did pedestrian crossings, a very necessary addition. In the 1930s, one of the last apple orchards could still be seen on Hookhills (P2030, page 84, right).

The final transformation was completed in 1966 when the dream of a bigger and better Public Hall or Summer Pavilion was finally achieved: the new Festival Hall Theatre opened on 10 June 1967 with a dazzling production of the Black and White Minstrels Show, which received a standing ovation.

Above right: Torbay Road c1965 P2044

Right: Torbay Road from the Rock Garden c1955 P2005

Far right: The Esplanade from Roundham Cabbage Fields 1890 25903

Left: **Deller's Café 1928** 58417A

Below Left: **Deller's Summer Café 1928** 81153A

Below Right: **The Devon Coast Country Club c1965** P2032

This was a prisoner of war camp during World War II, then a holiday camp. It is now a housing estate.

So, except for the Victorian ladies' voluminous black dresses, men's bowler hats, knitted bathing costumes and the lack of freedom to bathe where you liked with whom you liked, dressed as you like, there is little difference in Paignton's watering place today. The seaside holiday, after all, is still an ice cream, a cup of tea, a photograph of the children on Donkey Daniel's ride, Punch and Judy on the soft golden sand, the annual Children's Week competitions (P2043, page 84) and plenty of good entertainment.

Perhaps a little of the old medieval fair spirit still lingers in all of us when that first firework goes up over the Regatta fair and we know that the summer season is once more drawing to a close!

Above: The Windmill, The Entrance to the Promenade c1955   P2012

A welcome to Paignton was still apparent when in 1955 a replica of one of the town's many 19th-century windmills was used as the rock garden centrepiece. To the left of the garden is the ageing tent-cum-Summer Pavilion, where John Berryman's 'Evening Stars' started to twinkle.

Opposite top: The Three Beaches and St George's Church from Hookhills c1950   P2030

Opposite below: The Pier c1965   P2043

This photograph shows pavement artists' squares ready for Children's Week competitions, and new Promenade lighting. The pier is somewhat changed, and now houses pin-tables, ghost rides and go-karts.

Above: **The Esplanade and the Pier 1896** 38561

Below: **The Sands and the Pier c1955** P2001

These last two photographs show Paignton then and now. For over a 100 years the Victorian venture has changed little in its outward appearance. It is sad that the enterprise led to the loss of Paignton's rolling green hills and marshland habitats, the many apple orchards and most of the cob cottages (although one or two are left, and can still be found if you know where to look). However, Paignton is fortunate, for it has the Paignton Preservation and Local History Society, which is doing its utmost to preserve what is left of this great Victorian adventure.

Index

Frith Book Co Titles

www.francisfrith.co.uk

The Frith Book Company publishes over 100 new titles each year. A selection of those currently available are listed below. For latest catalogue please contact Frith Book Co.

Town Books 96 pages, approx 100 photos. County and Themed Books 128 pages, approx 150 photos (unless specified). All titles hardback laminated case and jacket except those indicated pb (paperback)

Amersham, Chesham & Rickmansworth (pb)	1-85937-340-2	£9.99
Ancient Monuments & Stone Circles	1-85937-143-4	£17.99
Aylesbury (pb)	1-85937-227-9	£9.99
Bakewell	1-85937-113-2	£12.99
Barnstaple (pb)	1-85937-300-3	£9.99
Bath (pb)	1-85937419-0	£9.99
Bedford (pb)	1-85937-205-8	£9.99
Berkshire (pb)	1-85937-191-4	£9.99
Berkshire Churches	1-85937-170-1	£17.99
Blackpool (pb)	1-85937-382-8	£9.99
Bognor Regis (pb)	1-85937-431-x	£9.99
Bournemouth	1-85937-067-5	£12.99
Bradford (pb)	1-85937-204-x	£9.99
Brighton & Hove(pb)	1-85937-192-2	£8.99
Bristol (pb)	1-85937-264-3	£9.99
British Life A Century Ago (pb)	1-85937-213-9	£9.99
Buckinghamshire (pb)	1-85937-200-7	£9.99
Camberley (pb)	1-85937-222-8	£9.99
Cambridge (pb)	1-85937-422-0	£9.99
Cambridgeshire (pb)	1-85937-420-4	£9.99
Canals & Waterways (pb)	1-85937-291-0	£9.99
Canterbury Cathedral (pb)	1-85937-179-5	£9.99
Cardiff (pb)	1-85937-093-4	£9.99
Carmarthenshire	1-85937-216-3	£14.99
Chelmsford (pb)	1-85937-310-0	£9.99
Cheltenham (pb)	1-85937-095-0	£9.99
Cheshire (pb)	1-85937-271-6	£9.99
Chester	1-85937-090-x	£12.99
Chesterfield	1-85937-378-x	£9.99
Chichester (pb)	1-85937-228-7	£9.99
Colchester (pb)	1-85937-188-4	£8.99
Cornish Coast	1-85937-163-9	£14.99
Cornwall (pb)	1-85937-229-5	£9.99
Cornwall Living Memories	1-85937-248-1	£14.99
Cotswolds (pb)	1-85937-230-9	£9.99
Cotswolds Living Memories	1-85937-255-4	£14.99
County Durham	1-85937-123-x	£14.99
Croydon Living Memories	1-85937-162-0	£9.99
Cumbria	1-85937-101-9	£14.99
Dartmoor	1-85937-145-0	£14.99
Derby (pb)	1-85937-367-4	£9.99
Derbyshire (pb)	1-85937-196-5	£9.99
Devon (pb)	1-85937-297-x	£9.99
Dorset (pb)	1-85937-269-4	£9.99
Dorset Churches	1-85937-172-8	£17.99
Dorset Coast (pb)	1-85937-299-6	£9.99
Dorset Living Memories	1-85937-210-4	£14.99
Down the Severn	1-85937-118-3	£14.99
Down the Thames (pb)	1-85937-278-3	£9.99
Down the Trent	1-85937-311-9	£14.99
Dublin (pb)	1-85937-231-7	£9.99
East Anglia (pb)	1-85937-265-1	£9.99
East London	1-85937-080-2	£14.99
East Sussex	1-85937-130-2	£14.99
Eastbourne	1-85937-061-6	£12.99
Edinburgh (pb)	1-85937-193-0	£8.99
England in the 1880s	1-85937-331-3	£17.99
English Castles (pb)	1-85937-434-4	£9.99
English Country Houses	1-85937-161-2	£17.99
Essex (pb)	1-85937-270-8	£9.99
Exeter	1-85937-126-4	£12.99
Exmoor	1-85937-132-9	£14.99
Falmouth	1-85937-066-7	£12.99
Folkestone (pb)	1-85937-124-8	£9.99
Glasgow (pb)	1-85937-190-6	£9.99
Gloucestershire	1-85937-102-7	£14.99
Great Yarmouth (pb)	1-85937-426-3	£9.99
Greater Manchester (pb)	1-85937-266-x	£9.99
Guildford (pb)	1-85937-410-7	£9.99
Hampshire (pb)	1-85937-279-1	£9.99
Hampshire Churches (pb)	1-85937-207-4	£9.99
Harrogate	1-85937-423-9	£9.99
Hastings & Bexhill (pb)	1-85937-131-0	£9.99
Heart of Lancashire (pb)	1-85937-197-3	£9.99
Helston (pb)	1-85937-214-7	£9.99
Hereford (pb)	1-85937-175-2	£9.99
Herefordshire	1-85937-174-4	£14.99
Hertfordshire (pb)	1-85937-247-3	£9.99
Horsham (pb)	1-85937-432-8	£9.99
Humberside	1-85937-215-5	£14.99
Hythe, Romney Marsh & Ashford	1-85937-256-2	£9.99

Available from your local bookshop or from the publisher

Frith Book Co Titles (continued)

Ipswich (pb)	1-85937-424-7	£9.99	St Ives (pb)	1-85937415-8	£9.99
Ireland (pb)	1-85937-181-7	£9.99	Scotland (pb)	1-85937-182-5	£9.99
Isle of Man (pb)	1-85937-268-6	£9.99	Scottish Castles (pb)	1-85937-323-2	£9.99
Isles of Scilly	1-85937-136-1	£14.99	Sevenoaks & Tunbridge	1-85937-057-8	£12.99
Isle of Wight (pb)	1-85937-429-8	£9.99	Sheffield, South Yorks (pb)	1-85937-267-8	£9.99
Isle of Wight Living Memories	1-85937-304-6	£14.99	Shrewsbury (pb)	1-85937-325-9	£9.99
Kent (pb)	1-85937-189-2	£9.99	Shropshire (pb)	1-85937-326-7	£9.99
Kent Living Memories	1-85937-125-6	£14.99	Somerset	1-85937-153-1	£14.99
Lake District (pb)	1-85937-275-9	£9.99	South Devon Coast	1-85937-107-8	£14.99
Lancaster, Morecambe & Heysham (pb)	1-85937-233-3	£9.99	South Devon Living Memories	1-85937-168-x	£14.99
Leeds (pb)	1-85937-202-3	£9.99	South Hams	1-85937-220-1	£14.99
Leicester	1-85937-073-x	£12.99	Southampton (pb)	1-85937-427-1	£9.99
Leicestershire (pb)	1-85937-185-x	£9.99	Southport (pb)	1-85937-425-5	£9.99
Lincolnshire (pb)	1-85937-433-6	£9.99	Staffordshire	1-85937-047-0	£12.99
Liverpool & Merseyside (pb)	1-85937-234-1	£9.99	Stratford upon Avon	1-85937-098-5	£12.99
London (pb)	1-85937-183-3	£9.99	Suffolk (pb)	1-85937-221-x	£9.99
Ludlow (pb)	1-85937-176-0	£9.99	Suffolk Coast	1-85937-259-7	£14.99
Luton (pb)	1-85937-235-x	£9.99	Surrey (pb)	1-85937-240-6	£9.99
Maidstone	1-85937-056-x	£14.99	Sussex (pb)	1-85937-184-1	£9.99
Manchester (pb)	1-85937-198-1	£9.99	Swansea (pb)	1-85937-167-1	£9.99
Middlesex	1-85937-158-2	£14.99	Tees Valley & Cleveland	1-85937-211-2	£14.99
New Forest	1-85937-128-0	£14.99	Thanet (pb)	1-85937-116-7	£9.99
Newark (pb)	1-85937-366-6	£9.99	Tiverton (pb)	1-85937-178-7	£9.99
Newport, Wales (pb)	1-85937-258-9	£9.99	Torbay	1-85937-063-2	£12.99
Newquay (pb)	1-85937-421-2	£9.99	Truro	1-85937-147-7	£12.99
Norfolk (pb)	1-85937-195-7	£9.99	Victorian and Edwardian Cornwall	1-85937-252-x	£14.99
Norfolk Living Memories	1-85937-217-1	£14.99	Victorian & Edwardian Devon	1-85937-253-8	£14.99
Northamptonshire	1-85937-150-7	£14.99	Victorian & Edwardian Kent	1-85937-149-3	£14.99
Northumberland Tyne & Wear (pb)	1-85937-281-3	£9.99	Vic & Ed Maritime Album	1-85937-144-2	£17.99
North Devon Coast	1-85937-146-9	£14.99	Victorian and Edwardian Sussex	1-85937-157-4	£14.99
North Devon Living Memories	1-85937-261-9	£14.99	Victorian & Edwardian Yorkshire	1-85937-154-x	£14.99
North London	1-85937-206-6	£14.99	Victorian Seaside	1-85937-159-0	£17.99
North Wales (pb)	1-85937-298-8	£9.99	Villages of Devon (pb)	1-85937-293-7	£9.99
North Yorkshire (pb)	1-85937-236-8	£9.99	Villages of Kent (pb)	1-85937-294-5	£9.99
Norwich (pb)	1-85937-194-9	£8.99	Villages of Sussex (pb)	1-85937-295-3	£9.99
Nottingham (pb)	1-85937-324-0	£9.99	Warwickshire (pb)	1-85937-203-1	£9.99
Nottinghamshire (pb)	1-85937-187-6	£9.99	Welsh Castles (pb)	1-85937-322-4	£9.99
Oxford (pb)	1-85937-411-5	£9.99	West Midlands (pb)	1-85937-289-9	£9.99
Oxfordshire (pb)	1-85937-430-1	£9.99	West Sussex	1-85937-148-5	£14.99
Peak District (pb)	1-85937-280-5	£9.99	West Yorkshire (pb)	1-85937-201-5	£9.99
Penzance	1-85937-069-1	£12.99	Weymouth (pb)	1-85937-209-0	£9.99
Peterborough (pb)	1-85937-219-8	£9.99	Wiltshire (pb)	1-85937-277-5	£9.99
Piers	1-85937-237-6	£17.99	Wiltshire Churches (pb)	1-85937-171-x	£9.99
Plymouth	1-85937-119-1	£12.99	Wiltshire Living Memories	1-85937-245-7	£14.99
Poole & Sandbanks (pb)	1-85937-251-1	£9.99	Winchester (pb)	1-85937-428-x	£9.99
Preston (pb)	1-85937-212-0	£9.99	Windmills & Watermills	1-85937-242-2	£17.99
Reading (pb)	1-85937-238-4	£9.99	Worcester (pb)	1-85937-165-5	£9.99
Romford (pb)	1-85937-319-4	£9.99	Worcestershire	1-85937-152-3	£14.99
Salisbury (pb)	1-85937-239-2	£9.99	York (pb)	1-85937-199-x	£9.99
Scarborough (pb)	1-85937-379-8	£9.99	Yorkshire (pb)	1-85937-186-8	£9.99
St Albans (pb)	1-85937-341-0	£9.99	Yorkshire Living Memories	1-85937-166-3	£14.99

See Frith books on the internet www.francisfrith.co.uk

FRITH PRODUCTS & SERVICES

Francis Frith would doubtless be pleased to know that the pioneering publishing venture he started in 1860 still continues today. A hundred and forty years later, The Francis Frith Collection continues in the same innovative tradition and is now one of the foremost publishers of vintage photographs in the world. Some of the current activities include:

Interior Decoration

Today Frith's photographs can be seen framed and as giant wall murals in thousands of pubs, restaurants, hotels, banks, retail stores and other public buildings throughout the country. In every case they enhance the unique local atmosphere of the places they depict and provide reminders of gentler days in an increasingly busy and frenetic world.

Product Promotions

Frith products are used by many major companies to promote the sales of their own products or to reinforce their own history and heritage. Frith promotions have been used by Hovis bread, Courage beers, Scots Porage Oats, Colman's mustard, Cadbury's foods, Mellow Birds coffee, Dunhill pipe tobacco, Guinness, and Bulmer's Cider.

Genealogy and Family History

As the interest in family history and roots grows world-wide, more and more people are turning to Frith's photographs of Great Britain for images of the towns, villages and streets where their ancestors lived; and, of course, photographs of the churches and chapels where their ancestors were christened, married and buried are an essential part of every genealogy tree and family album.

Frith Products

All Frith photographs are available Framed or just as Mounted Prints and Posters (size 23 x 16 inches). These may be ordered from the address below. From time to time other products - Address Books, Calendars, Table Mats, etc - are available.

The Internet

Already twenty thousand Frith photographs can be viewed and purchased on the internet through the Frith websites and a myriad of partner sites.

For more detailed information on Frith companies and products, look at these sites:

www.francisfrith.co.uk
www.francisfrith.com
(for North American visitors)

See the complete list of Frith Books at:

www.francisfrith.co.uk

This web site is regularly updated with the latest list of publications from the Frith Book Company. If you wish to buy books relating to another part of the country that your local bookshop does not stock, you may purchase on-line.

For further information, trade, or author enquiries please contact us at the address below:
The Francis Frith Collection, Frith's Barn, Teffont, Salisbury, Wiltshire, England SP3 5QP.
Tel: +44 (0)1722 716 376 Fax: +44 (0)1722 716 881 Email: sales@francisfrith.co.uk

See Frith books on the internet www.francisfrith.co.uk